beginning to see
慧眼初開

by sujata
pen-art by julio lynch
translated into Chinese
by Cheng Chen-huang

蘇吉達／文
藍吉利／圖
鄭振煌／譯

this book is dedicated to

the 9 to 5ers.
and everybody else

謹以.本書獻給

朝九晚五的上班族
和全體人類

a collection of epigrams
about the problem
of living

and the freedom
to be gained
through meditation

人　　生　　雋　　語

禪　　定　　自　　在

much suffering
comes into the
life of one who
tries to be any-
where but
here
in the present
moment

捨近求諸遠
不在當下一刻
用功的人
眾苦紛至。

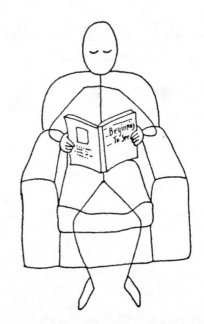

are you
content
with where you
are right now ?

你滿意
當下的你嗎？

because "right nows" are all you have

因為「當下」是你所能擁有的一切。

there is nothing
in this life that we can
have for very long

人生無常，
朝聚夕散。……

things and people
come ...
        then leave us ...

世事滄桑，
生住異滅。……

and we are left
sad and aching
because of
our
attachment

我們因爲
執著，
而有悲傷痛苦。

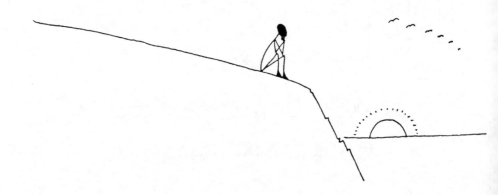

because we are only
accepting of pleasure
in our lives

因爲我們
只接受快樂，

在我們
閃避痛苦的時候，
就產生無量的恐懼。

an immense
amount of fear
is created as
we spend our
lives dodging
pain

an immense amount
of fear is created
as we spend our lives
dodging pain

在我們
閃避痛苦的時候，
就產生無量的恐懼。

在我們
閃避痛苦的時候，
就產生無量的恐懼。

an immense amount
of fear is created
as we spend our
lives dodging pain

the world continually
demands that we
direct our
attention
outside
ourselves

世界一直在
要求我們
把注意力
投向身外。

meditation teaches
us to revolt

坐禪却教我們
反過來，

and turn that
awareness toward
our neglected
dimly-lit
insides ...

把覺醒
投向
被我們忽視的、
昏闇的內心。

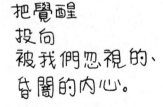

Painful feelings*
in the mind indicate
wrong attitudes
about life

心中的
痛苦感覺*，
表示我們的
人生態度錯誤。

a meditation
retreat can show
us what we're
doing wrong

坐禪可以
告訴我們：
我們做錯了什麼。

*jealousy, envy, hatred, loneliness, frustration, depression

*嫉妒、羨慕、瞋恨、孤獨、挫折、沮喪

we live our
lives fearfully

我們在
恐懼中過日子

to such an extent
that we live
dishonestly

讓我們
丂由得
自欺欺人。

there is dishonesty
in any mind
which demands
that reality
occur in a
specific way

每個人都不老實，

以致大家

都不按事實出牌。

we progress in this
life according to our
honest wisdom.

我們這一生，
因有誠實的智慧而成長。

honest wisdom is
realizing what you feel,
knowing what you think,

誠實的智慧，就是
了了分明你的覺受，
了了分明你的思惟，

and opening
your attention
to everything
which comes
before you.

並把你的注意力
專注在眼前的
每一件事上。

we should take
time each day to
understand
ourselves

每天我們都必須
抽點時間
來了解自己，

to watch exactly
what we experience
in walking and sitting
meditation.

來如實觀察
我們在行禪
　和坐禪中
的經驗。

how to
start a
good day

如何開始美好的一天？

every day you are
responsible
for how you feel

no one can make you
unhappy

or nervous

每一天你都要

為自己的感覺負責

誰都不能讓你

不快樂

或緊張

choices in a
meditator's life are
very simple :

禪行者的
生活抉擇
很簡單：

he does those
things which contribute
to his awareness

凡所作爲
要有助於
覺醒

he refrains from
things which do not

絕不做
有礙覺醒的事。

Choose

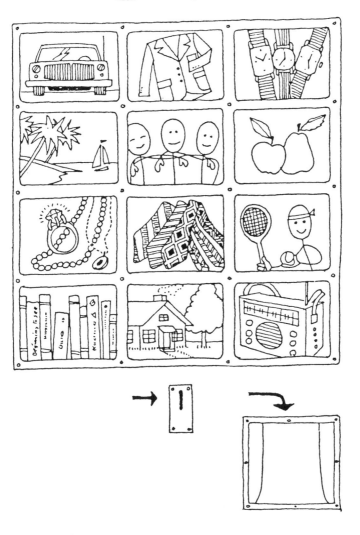

the first step in
spiritual growth is to
do what we love to do
and to become
aware of doing it

修行的第一步是：
做我們
　喜歡做的事，
而且要
　　了了分明。

in what direction
are you taking yourself?
(is it worth your effort?
is it exactly where
you want
  to go?)

Coolsville 清涼村

Worryhollow 憂愁谷

Fun City 歡樂城

Worktown 工作鎮

Twinkyland 微笑市

Restrooms 廁所

你要把自己
帶往那個方向?
(值得你這麼做嗎?
確是你所嚮往
  的地方嗎?)

insight meditation
systematically trains us
to be aware of every-
thing "we're up to"

觀禪
有系統的訓練我們
了了分明
「我們所面對的」一切

the mind is only a
sophisticated
mirror

心只是一面
複雜的
鏡子

it is what it sees
it is what it sees

它看到什麼就是什麼
它看到什麼就是什麼

be careful what
you show it
because
you can be

小心你怎麼
表現它,因為
你可能

anything
anything
anything
anything

無所不是
無所不是
無所不是
無所不是

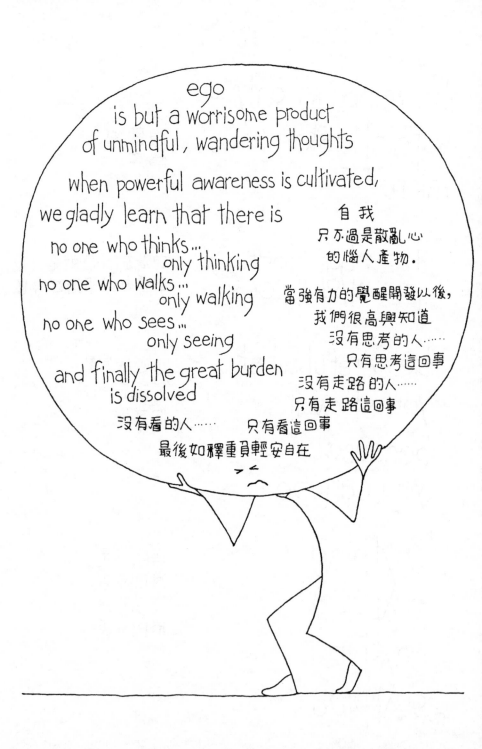

detached
does not mean
dead

rather, it is made of
lovingkindness
Compassion
Sympathetic joy
and
equanimity

万, 執著
並 非
死 亡

而 是
慈 悲
喜 捨

one of the
highest blessings is
a friend with whom
we can respond
openly and freely

人　　生
最大的福氣是
擁有一位
我們可以
袒裎相見、推心置腹
的朋友

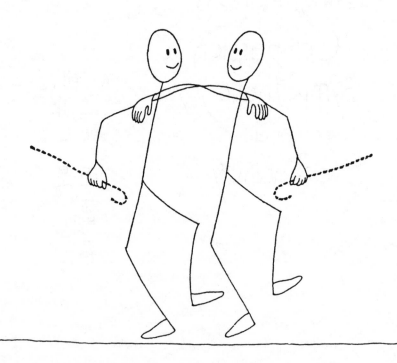

it is hard
to be constantly
loving

but it is
harder
to be
unloving

常　保
慈　悲　心
難

但
心懷瞋恚
更　難

this living is
so hard
how can we
be anything
but loving?

    besides teaching insight meditation the buddha
also taught a meditation to develop loving kindness
for all creatures — he instructed that we sit in
a quiet place and reflect first on the dangers of
hatred, anger and resentment, and the benefits of
loving kindness — these reflections remind us of
the importance of maintaining a loving attitude
in all circumstances and give us energy for the
meditation.
    because only when there is love for one-
self can there be love for others, we first practice
loving kindness towards ourselves by thinking of
our own good qualities and kind actions —
warmth for ourselves grows as we repeat over
and over the loving thought : 'may I be free
from my troubles (anger, fear, tension, anxiety,
hatred, etc.) may I live happily.'
    when we first begin the practice of loving-
kindness, we may be surprised to find that we
have difficulty in reflecting on our good qualities
— we may feel shy or guilty in thinking of
ourselves in such a positive way, or there
may be self-hatred conditioned in our minds
by years of comparing ourselves with others
or with some ideal to which we might cling.
    when we begin practice, it may be help-
ful to start each period of practice by writing
down a few reflections to help us focus our
attention.
    for example, one day our reflections
might be:

此生
舉步維艱，
我們
怎能不
慈悲爲懷？

　　佛陀除了教我們智慧的禪觀以外，還
教我們慈悲的禪觀－－他要我們靜居晏坐，首先
觀想瞋恨的危險和慈悲的利益－－如此觀想，
可以策勵我們常懷慈悲、精進坐禪。

　　自愛才能愛別人，我們應先想到自己的
好品質和善行－－念念發願「離苦（憤怒、恐懼、
緊張、焦慮、憎恨等）得樂」長養菩提道心。

　　開始修慈悲行時，可能會觀想不起來
自己的好品質－－觀想自己如此積善行善，也許
會覺得汗顏或罪惡；由於多年來與別人或我
們所嚮往的理想作比較，心中也不覺會自怨
自哀。

　　修慈悲行時，最好寫下觀想的要點，以
幫助我們一心繫念。

　　例如，我們可以觀想：

dangers of hatred and resentment

1- makes me fearful
2- creates restlessness and agitation
3- makes me feel miserable
4- makes me critical and hard on myself

advantages of lovingkindness

1- makes my mind clear
2- frees my body of tension
3- makes me feel good about myself
4- makes it easier to be with others

my own good qualities

1- I try to be patient
2- I am willing to change and grow
3- I want to be more loving
4- I have pretty toes

spend some time each day writing and reflecting in this way - then spend the last ten minutes of the meditation time specifically cultivating that warm and open space which thoughts of lovingkindness produce, by gently and silently repeating your own wish for yourself : 'may I be loving' or 'may I be free from restlessness' or 'may I be free from anxiety,' in whatever way feels appropriate for you.

if we work ardently at this meditation we will begin to see a healthy change happening within ourselves.

in time, when loving thoughts flow freely for ourselves, the lovingkindness may be extended to all beings everywhere without distinction —

may all beings be happy.

瞋恨的危險
1. 使自己心生恐懼
2. 使自己焦慮不安
3. 使自己自憐自哀
4. 使自己苛責自己

慈悲的好處
1. 使自己心靈澄澈
2. 使自己放鬆自在
3. 使自己自尊自重
4. 使自己廣結人緣

我的好品質
1. 我要忍耐
2. 我要改變和成長
3. 我要更加慈悲
4. 我有美麗的腳趾頭

　　每天就花些時間這麼寫,這麼觀想——然後利用靜坐時間的最後十分鐘,柔和而靜靜地重複你對自己的發願:「願我慈悲為懷」、「願我無憂無慮」、「願我輕安自在」,悠遊任運,一無滯礙。如此,慈悲的思想將可使你安祥而清明。

　　如此精進觀禪,我們本身必然會有健康的蛻變。

　　心中常懷慈悲,一切眾生將感同身受——願一切眾生離苦得樂。

anger is most
dangerous

it destroys you,
the person next
to you,
and the place where
you live

瞋心最危險，
火燒功德林。

它會毀滅你、
你周圍的人
和你居住的地方。

when aversion arises in
our minds,
we must either mindfully
drop it
or start communicating

瞋念起時，
應立刻息怒
或開始溝通。

hatred
is a crime
 in any of its forms --
  resentment, aversion,
  jealousy, anger, harshness,
    disgust --

瞋
不管是 --
憎恨、嫌棄、
嫉妒、發怒、
粗暴或厭惡
-- 都是
 一種罪惡。

if we watch carefully
 what it does to our
 feelings and what we do
to other peoples feelings
when motivated by it, we
 have no choice but to
  give it up

如果我們能夠
 仔細觀察
瞋心對我們的傷害、
 對別人的傷害，
則除了捨棄之外，
 別無選擇。

we are very empty inside
just watch us work to fill
up the vacant hours

只要看看
我們在閒暇時
如何不甘寂寞，

就知道
我們的
內心
多空虛了。

time on our
hands is very
dangerous

we might stop long
enough to notice that
we are very unhappy
people
going nowhere
special ....

時間
在我們手上
非常危險
我們應多花點時間
想一想
我們是很丕快樂的
人
茫無目標 ----

the buddha did not
come in the 6th
century b.c.

to reassure us
that
the world was
moving in the
right
direction

佛一直到
西元前第六世紀
才示現於世
他苦口婆心地
告訴我們
世界是沿著
正確的
方向
移動

Once a King who was
marching to war came near
the place where an enlightened teacher was living.
the King was in a great
hurry but he wanted to learn
something from the saint-
respectfully the King approached,
paid homage, and asked the
holy one:
"will you tell me the buddha's
teachings, for I have little time and
may even be killed this
very day"
the sage looked upon the
man in the royal cloak and answered
with but one word:
"awareness"

從前有一位國王
率領大軍奔赴沙場，
來到一位覺者住的
地方。
他戎馬倥傯，
却不忘
向聖者請教。
他恭恭敬敬地
走向聖者，
禮拜，
而後問道：
「我的時間不多，
朝不保夕，
也許今天就葬身馬蹄下，
因此，請告訴我
佛法是什麼？」
聖者望著
威風凜凜的國王，
只回答二個字：
"覺 醒"。

meditation is
for those who are
born without having
it all together

精神不能集中的
人
應該學習
坐禪

mindfully attending to the sensation
of the breath -
a tranquility and
insight exersise -

對呼吸
觀照得明明了了，
就是一種
止觀的練習；

is politically, economically
and spiritually
the practice
of
peacefulness

可以獲得政治上、
經濟上和精神上的
安詳。

meditation is not straining
or striving

it is a relaxation

坐禪　　　不可以緊繃著絃
也不可以企求什麼

它是一種放鬆

the back should be straight not tense

背挺直
但不可以緊張

an insight
meditation exercise

for the development of clear, mindful awareness, the buddha taught us to observe closely the movements of the body and the mind. a good way to develop your attentiveness, concentration and insight is to watch carefully the rising and falling of the abdomen. in this meditation exercise we begin by observing these obvious bodily movements. when these become clear we will also be able to be aware of the more subtle movements of the mind.

go to a quiet place and sit in a comfortable position with eyes closed and back straight but not rigid. the movement of the abdomen is always present: place your attention on its natural in and out movement, making a mental note of each part of the process as it is occurring. it is not necessary to verbally repeat the words, "rising" and "falling", or even to think of "rising" and "falling" in the form of words. instead, only be aware of the actual process of rising and falling. as you become more and more alert and can follow the movements more carefully, you will become aware that the breathing is sometimes shallow, sometimes deep, sometimes rapid, sometimes slow and calm. these variations

觀禪
練習

　　佛陀教我們仔細觀照身心的動作，以發展清明而專注的覺醒。發展注意力、專注和智慧的好方法，便是小心觀察腹部的起伏。首先，我們要觀察明顯的身體動作，當我們對身體動作能夠了了分明時，也就可以對比較細膩的心理動作了了分明。

　　找一個安靜的地方，用舒適的姿勢坐下來，閉上眼睛，背脊挺直而不僵硬。腹部的動作要觀察得清清楚楚：注意腹部的自然起伏，心中要記住整個過程的每一細節。不必發聲念「起」、「伏」，甚至也不必想到「起」、「伏」。反之，只要對起伏的實際動作了了分明就可以。當你變得越來越清醒，能夠比較仔細地觀照腹部的起伏時，你就可以明白呼吸有時候是淺的，有時候是深的，有時候是急促的，有時候是緩慢而寧靜的。這些差異

should be noted, however there should be no effort to control or to interfere with the breathing in any way. just choicelessly watch the movements as they appear when you are breathing normally.

while you are watching the rise and fall of the abdomen, the mind may, by itself, go towards other objects, such as thoughts, feelings, bodily sensations. these new objects should be noted as soon as they arise. if a thought comes to your mind, be aware of "thinking". if a sound comes to your attention, make a mental note of "hearing." after each such note, firmly and calmly return your attention to the primary objects of meditation, the movements of the abdomen.

as you develop more concentration on the primary objects, you will quickly notice any other object as it arises. however, until the mind is alert enough to notice these objects as soon as they arise, it will tend to wander unmindfully after these thoughts, feelings and emotions. sometime later, the meditator becomes aware that he has been day dreaming. as soon as one is aware that his attention has drifted away from the present moment, he should patiently note that his mind has been "wandering" and that he is now "remembering to be mindful". then one should lovingly return the attention to watching

必須加以注意，但絕不可以刻意想控制或干涉呼吸。以平常心觀照呼吸，順其自然。

　　當你在觀察腹部的起伏時，你的心也許會散亂，如思想、感覺、感受等。心一亂，就要立刻注意。如果心中起了妄想，你就要知道你正在「妄想」。如果聲音引起你的注意力，你就要知道你在「聽」。然後，你就把注意力回復到觀照的最初目標——腹部的起伏上。

　　當你能夠比較專注地觀照腹部的起伏時，心一起妄念就可以立刻發現。不過，除非你的心能夠清醒到一有妄念就立刻覺察時，你仍將心猿意馬，妄念紛飛。不久，禪行者將知道自己一直在做白日夢。只要你知道你的心已經亂了，你就要耐著性子注意你已經「迷失」了，然後「記得要專注」。如此，你將愉快地重新觀照腹部的起伏。

the rising and falling.

mindfulness can also be practiced during walking meditation, with the lifting, placing and putting of the foot as the primary objects of awareness. with head upright, keeping your eyes on the ground about six feet ahead, walk at a moderately slow pace, with steps small enough so that, without losing your balance, you can place one foot firmly on the ground before moving the next foot. remember to note each part of the movement as it occurs. it is a good idea to spend equal amounts of time in walking and in sitting meditation --- for example, thirty minutes of walking, then thirty of sitting, later, one hour of walking, then one hour of sitting.

during all movements and activities of the day --- eating, washing, moving from place to place, job to job --- one should be aware of the movements of the body necessary for each activity, or of any thought, feeling or physical sensation which arises predominately.

one who persists in noting all objects as they come to his attention will develop increasingly clear awareness. noting should be done neither too fast nor too slowly. It should be immediate, firm and clear, but not harsh. one is not to be lazy and sit day dreaming, but

行禪也可以訓練專注，這時候就要觀照腳的舉起、移動和放下。抬起頭，眼睛看著前方六呎的地面，步伐要慢而輕，步子要小，以保持平衡。第一隻腳要穩穩地踩下後，才可以再移動第二隻腳，記住你要知道你是在走路。行禪和坐禪交換練習，是一個很好的方法，……，譬如，三十分鐘行禪，然後三十分鐘坐禪，然後再一個小時行禪，一個小時坐禪。

　　在白天的一切動作和活動中，不管是吃飯、洗臉、走路或工作，都要對你的身體動作了了分明；當心中起了妄念、感覺或覺受時，也要清清楚楚。

　　如果你能夠知道你在注意些什麼，就可以不斷發展清明的覺醒。觀照時，要不急不緩，卻必須即時、肯定而清晰，不能粗糙。你不可以偷懶，盡作白日夢，

rather to develop an awareness of the objects which is accepting and alert. at a certain point when the mindfulness is well developed, awareness will be automatic, and there will be less and less need for making mental notes. however, whenever attention weakens, one should return to making clear notes.

it would be convenient if one could simply "decide" to be aware . however, we are conditioned not to be aware . our minds are trained to be complicated , and so it is necessary to re-train ourselves in order to be simply aware . the most skillful way for a beginning meditator to develop mindful awareness is to place himself under the guidance of a qualified meditation teacher for a period of intense practice . during a meditation retreat one leaves behind for a time the rush and trouble of his daily life, and in an atmosphere of quiet mindfulness and lovingkindness, devotes his energy entirely to the development of awareness. the minimum length of time usually needed for beginning westerners is one month . after completing such a period of intensive meditation, one is better able to continue the development and practice of mindfulness in daily life .

你應該心攝萬物，清明覺醒。當你能夠一心繫念時，自然就會覺醒，漸漸也就不念而念了。不過，心一亂，就要立刻察知。

你只要「決定」想覺醒，就一切好辦了。不過，我們總是有罣礙，無法覺醒。我們的心被訓練得複雜萬端，因此，必須再訓練，以恢復覺醒。初機最好要跟禪師精進修行一段時間。閉關坐禪時，要萬緣放下，心境平和而慈悲為懷，全心全力發展覺醒。西方初學者通常需要一個月時間打好基礎，然後就可以隨時隨地修禪了。

what could be
better than a
meditation you
can take
anywhere?

行住坐臥，
無非是禪，
斯為無上
法門。

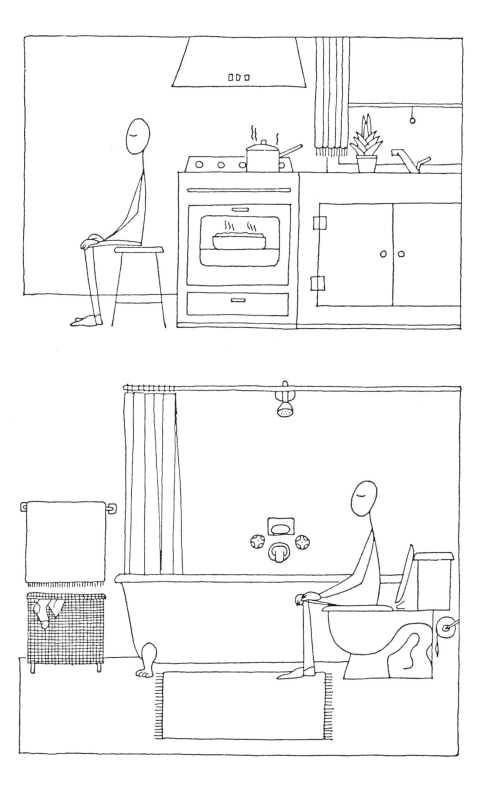

a saint is a very simple 聖人是非常單純的
man : 人：
    when he walks, he walks 當他走路時，他走路
    when he talks, he talks 當他說話時，他說話
    and thats all
he doesn't think while 當他聽時，他不.想.
    listening,
day dream while walking 當他走路時，
    see while touching 他不.做白日夢
    當他觸時，他不.看

that is very hard 那很難辦到
that is why he is a saint 那正是他為什麼
    是聖人的原因
that is why there is 那正是為什麼
trouble in our lives 人生多苦的原因

tension
is the first noble truth:

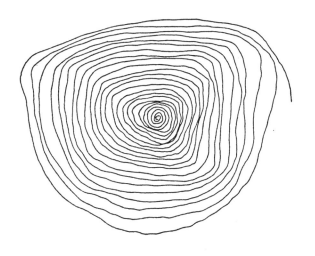

life is suffering

緊張是第一聖諦：生命是苦。

the price of
wisdom
is pain:

智慧的代價
是苦

but it is this wisdom
that cuts off
the suffering

但斷苦的
正是智慧

finally, there is
no choice but
to bleed freely

最後 別無
選擇 只能
自由地流血

Your pain can be
the breaking 你的痛苦也許是
of the shell 打破
which 你的
encloses 所知障
your
under-
standing

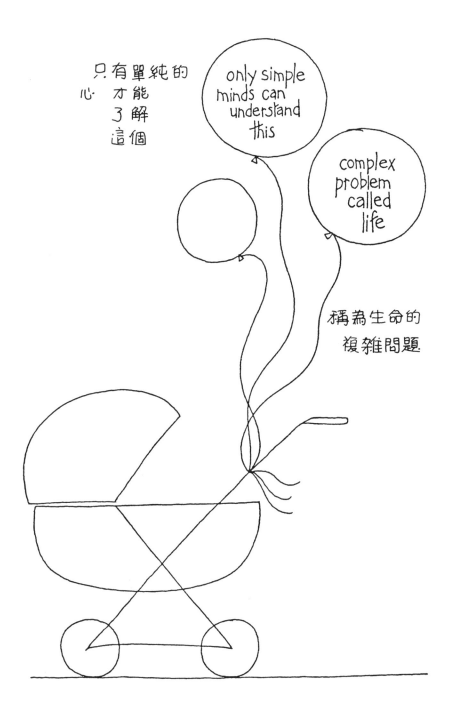

if we accept everything
in life as our
teacher

we will soon
be free

from the
pain of
unnecessary resistance
and
unnecessary desire

如果我們能夠
以萬物為
師

將可立即
免於

無謂的抗拒
和無謂的慾望
之苦。

We run here and there
all our lives
trying to be successful,
    correct and right

    when the
    goal
    of life
    is
    learning

在人生
目標的
學習
過程中
我們
恓恓惶惶
追求成功
完美無缺.

a meditation retreat
brings great relief because
for a time we don't have
to take our mind and its'
problems seriously,

精進坐禪會讓我們解脫自在，
因為這段期間我們不必太
用心，也不必太操心，

we don't have to act
upon its thousand wander-
ing thougts,

我們不必因妄念紛飛
而忙得暈頭轉向，

we just note them
mindfully and they pass
away‧‧‧‧‧‧‧‧‧‧‧

我們只是了了分明，
妄念隨起隨滅。

the untrained
mind is so
vulnerable to
Circumstances

something good
happens and it
is happy...

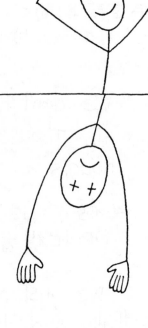

something bad
happens and it
is in pain...

妄心隨境轉
遇順境則喜
遇逆境則悲.

one who has sufficiently
suffered the attachments
and aversions of his mind's
uncontrolled wanderings
quickly becomes

watchful /◖◗/ of

any direction \◖◗\

in which /◖◗/

\◖◗\ the mind

/◖◗/ moves

深受妄念執著瞋恨之苦的人，
一入禪定，
就可以了知心的去向。

your mind has
a mind of its
own

(where
do
you
fit in?)

您的心
自有主張

(您把
心
安住
在那裏?)

thoughts are not
necessarily connected
with reality

that is why the
buddha taught us
to be aware
of them
before we are
influenced
by them

人的思想.
未必是發自
真如本性

那就是為什麼
佛陀要教我們
觀照思想.
免得受其影響

what happens between
the time we awake
and the time we
go to bed

is out
of our control

在我們
醒來之後，睡覺之前
所發生的一切
都万·是
我們所能控制的

bittersweet goes the life of him –
that clouded and distracted
stranger to reality
without awareness , he
stumbles and falls
he hurts himself to death

無明障蔽和思想紛亂的人
不識得真如本性
一輩子嚐盡甜酸苦辣.
愚昧.無知，跟跟蹌蹌
自己傷害自己 至死不悔

if living were an easy
thing to do
there would be no need
for mental training

但因生活
一帆風順

就沒有必要
修身養性了

but because life often
becomes very,
very hard

正因為世事多艱
洵非易與

we often have
to meditate
very, very
hard

所以.我們要
精進坐禪
不退不轉

the mind is the
only means we have
of getting out of
this mess

心是
跳出這個
泥淖的
唯一途徑

careful
with it

好好
修心·

immorality
    selfishness,
anger and
    chemicals
dull this single key

邪惡
    自私
嗔恨
    情緒
都會
使這把唯一的鑰匙
變得不靈光

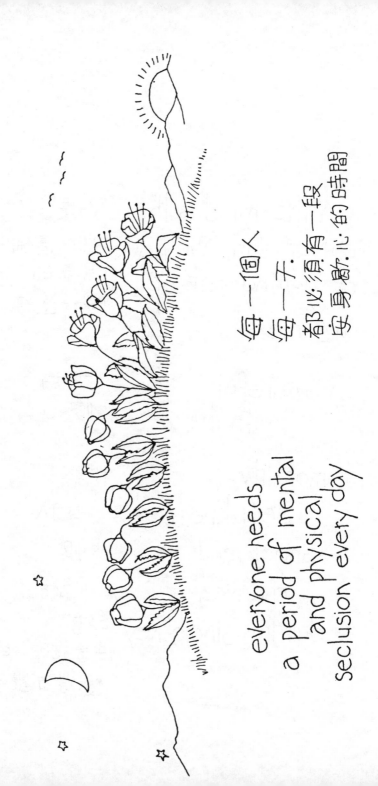

everyone heeds
a period of mental
and physical
seclusion every day

每一個人
每一天
都必須有一段
安身歇心的時間

meditating is
the kindest
thing we can
do for
ourselves

坐才單是
我們對待自己
最友善的
方式

our mind is a
garden
by selecting
what it thinks
upon,

we can grow
either
thorny weeds
or beautiful
tender flowers

心 就是一座
花園
我們想什麼

它 就長什麼
或 雜草叢生
或 鮮花滿園

(but even a
little weed
can learn
to grow
flowers)

(但即使是
一株雜草
也可以學習
開花)

reaching
enlightenment
is just a matter
of continuous
practice . . . . ※

證悟

只是

不斷修行的

結果. ～～～～～ ※

you can

do

it

你可以
做
得到

our characters are
developed by persistent practice

if we practice love
we become more loving

if we practice patience
we become more patient

if we practice generosity
we become more generous

我們的性格
可以由精進修行來培養
如果我們修持慈悲
就可以變得更慈悲
如果我們修持忍辱
就可以變得更能忍辱
如果我們修持布施
就可以變得更有能力布施

communication lovingkindness
insight into reality
form an interdependent
triangle :
neglect one and we
diminish the other two
practice one and all
are increased

觀照實相
構成一個互依互存的
三角形：
忽視其中一個
就減少其他兩個
修持一個
就增加所有三個

basically
life is unsatisfactory
because :

1. it is not perfect
2. we only get two weeks of vacation
    each year
3. our joys are impermanent
4. no one gets out alive
5. our bodies have to be washed over
    and over again

基本上
人生是苦的
因為
1. 人生有缺陷
2. 每年只有兩週假期
3. 我們的歡樂變化無常
4. 沒有人當生成就
5. 我們必須不斷洗澡

6. the freeway is crowded
7. we must be taught by pain as well as by pleasure
8. our name sounds dumb
9. we must argue that life is not unsatisfactory
10. most of our happiness depends on mere thoughts of the past and the future

6. 高速公路車滿為患
7. 我們必須從苦樂才能記取教訓
8. 我們的名字粗俗不雅
9. 我們必須辯論人生並不苦
10. 我們往往要沉緬過去和幻想未來才會覺得快樂

正 念.
放在
伸手可及的地方

take delight in mindfulness,
control your mind,
pull yourself
out of the mire of passions

以正念為樂
控制你的心
把你自己
從七情六慾
的泥淖中
拉出來.

as would an elephant
sunk in mud
come out of it

有如陷入泥中
的大象
能夠走出污泥

nothing is gained without effort
to train your mind, you have to work
every minute, every day, every year

from one life to another

天下沒有白吃的午餐
修行必須.
生生世世，年復一年
日復一日，分分秒秒
精進不懈

be kind and merciful
let no one ever come to you
without going away
better and happier

慈悲關懷
讓每一個來到你跟前的人
離開你時
能夠更美好 更快樂

mercy is the highest
attitude

慈悲是
至高無上的態度

one day a mother lost her only child. she went to the buddha in search of a remedy for her dead son, carrying the corpse. the buddha agreed to help her if she could bring to him a bag of white mustard seeds. however, she had to obtain these mustard seeds from a house where no member had ever died.

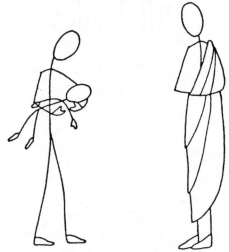

有一天，一位母親喪失了她的獨生子。她就捧著孩子的屍體，來到佛陀的跟前，請求佛陀給予補救。佛陀答應幫助她，如果她能夠帶回來一袋白芥子的話。不過她只能向那些家裏從來沒有死過人的人家要芥子。

the distraught mother went from one house to another asking if anyone had ever died in the house. the answer was always positive... here the grandfather died 3 years ago, - there the mother died by giving birth to her last child, etc... in every house she was told: "the living are few, but the dead are many".

這位傷心的媽媽，就挨家挨戶地問，是否有人曾經死過。答案都是肯定的。這家三年前死了祖父，那家的母親死於難產，每一家都是這麼告訴她:「活的人少，死的人多。」

after a while she understood the nature of life.
she returned to the buddha without the
mustard seeds . the buddha comforted her
explaining that death is common to all living
beings.
she understood that the life of human beings
flickers like the light of the lamp and she
finally stopped weeping and accepted the
death of her only son.

不久，她就知道了生命的性質。她兩手空空地回到了佛陀的面前，佛陀就安慰她，死是一切生物都免不了的。

　　她終於了解，人類的生命就像燈光般的閃爍不定，於是停止哭泣，接受她的獨生子去世的事實。

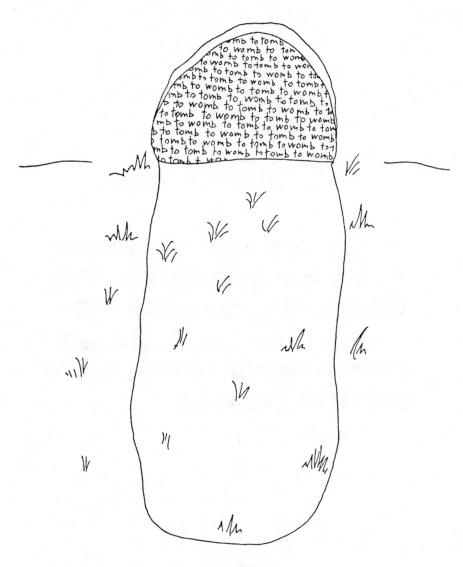

走向 墳 墓
走向 子宮 走向墳墓走向
子宮 走向墳墓走向子宮 走
向墳墓走向 子宮 走向墳墓走向
走向墳墓 走向子宮 走向
墳墓走向 子宮走向墳墓走向子宮

enlightment is an
alternative
to life, after life, after
life, after life, after
life, after life, after
life, after life, after life,
after life, after life, after life, after life, after life, after life, after life, after life, afte life, after life, after life

開悟是
生命的
另一個選擇，
來生，來
生，來生，來
生，來生，來
生，來生，來生
來生，來生，來生，來生，來生，來生，來生，來生，來生，來生，來生

During the time of the buddha, there was a young monk called nanda who did not understand the necessity for mindfulness. one day, nanda began to cherish the idea of giving his best robe to the enlightened teacher sangara. nanda was most infatuated with the idea, thinking that it would be an act of great merit to show such generosity towards a spiritually developed being.

he thought to himself, "by this noble deed, surely I will soon attain enlightment". because he was not yet well trained to mindfully watch the nature of his thoughts, nanda did not recognize the selfish desire and attachment which made his intentions impure.

the next day, the young monk waited until sangara left the monastery. in his absence, nanda swept his room, brought water for drinking and washing, prepared a seat for him of cushions and flowers, and laid out the gift of the robe. then nanda sat down and waited. when he saw sangara returning, he quickly went out the road, greeted him respectfully, and brought him to his quarters. seeing the room, the teacher was pleased with the young monks energy and kindness. nanda invited him to be seated on the prepared seat, gave him water to drink, bathed his feet. then nanda took a palm leaf and began to fan the holy one. he began the presentation of the gift, saying that he wanted with all his heart to give this, his best robe, to sangara.

the teacher detected that the young monk had not been mindful of his desires and had allowed

在佛陀的時代，有一位年輕的比丘，名叫難陀，他不了解正念的必要性。有一天，難陀比丘急著要把他最好的袈裟供養給開悟的老師僧伽羅。

這個念頭使難陀魂牽夢縈，他心裏頭想著，對一位修行到家的老師如此慷慨，功德必定很大。

他自言自語：「藉著這個高尚的行為，我必然很快就會開悟。」因為他的修行功夫還不夠，無法對思想的性質了了分明，認不出這是他的自私心和執著在作祟，使得他的意圖染污不淨。

第二天，這位年輕的比丘，在僧伽羅離開寺院之後，把房間打掃乾淨，端來飲用水和洗滌用的水，準備好坐墊和鮮花，鋪上他所要供養的袈裟。

然後，他就坐下來等，一看見僧伽羅回來，立刻跑到馬路上，恭迎老師到他的住處。老師看了房間之後，對於難陀的勤勞和虔誠，很是高興。

難陀請老師坐到墊子上，供養飲水，幫老師洗腳。然後，拿起棕櫚葉，替老師扇風。接著，獻上袈裟說，他要以全心全意供養老師。

老師發現這位年輕比丘並未照見自己的慾望，讓

himself to become attached to the idea of giving this gift . seeing this as an opportunity to teach nanda the danger of unmindfulness, the holy one replied that he already had a complete set of robes and as he had no need for the gift, instructed nanda to give the robe to some needy monk. at this nanda repeated his request several times, only to have the teacher thank him for offering the gift, but instruct him to give it elsewhere.

this polite refusal hurt nanda's feelings and resentment arose in his mind . in this clouded state of mind, he stood fanning the teacher. rather than practicing mindfulness by dismissing his resentment and attending to the fanning, nanda permitted his mind to dwell on the incident . as his mind wandered concerning the declined gift, his resentment grew, and he thought,

"if sangara is not willing to recieve my gift, why should I remain a monk ? I will become a householder once more". then his thoughts began to wander restlessly, taking his attention farther and farther from the present moment in which he stood fanning the teacher.

"suppose I become a householder once more", he thought, "how shall I earn a living ? I will sell this robe and buy myself a she-goat. as the she-goat brings forth young, I will sell them and in this way make a profit. when I have accumulated a profit, I will take a wife, and my wife will bear me a son. I will put my son in a little cart, and taking my son and wife along with me, I will make the journey back here to

自己執著於供養的念頭。老師認為因緣已經成熟了，應該把不能一心不亂的危險告訴難陀。

老師於是回答說，他已經有一套袈裟，並不需要這項供養，要求難陀把它轉送給其他比丘。難陀聽後，再三懇求，只希望老師能夠感謝他，想不到老師反而要他轉送給別人。

老師的婉拒，傷了難陀的心，於是心生憎恨。

雖然他還是站著替老師扇風，心中卻一片晦暗。他不以掃除憎恨和專心扇風來修習正念，卻讓心執著於這件事情上。一想到要供養袈裟而被拒絕，就起憎恨心，他想：

「如果僧伽羅不肯接受我的供養，為什麼我還必須當和尚？我要還俗。」他開始心煩氣躁，胡思亂想，忘了當時他正在替老師扇風。

「如果我還俗，」他盤算著：「我要如何維生？我將賣掉這件袈裟，買一隻母羊。母羊會生小羊，我把羊賣掉，就可以發財。

「錢積多了，就可以娶一房媳婦，太太將替我生個孩子，然後我要把孩子放在車內，帶著妻兒回來這裏，

pay respects to the elder sangara . as we travel,
I will say to my wife, "wife, bring my son, for I
wish to carry him . she will reply, " why
should you carry the boy ? you push the cart ".
saying this, she will take the boy in her arms,
thinking to carry him herself; but lacking the
necessary strength, she will let him fall in
the road and he will land in the path of the
wheels and the cart will run over him . then
I will say to her, "wife, you have ruined me".
so saying I will bring down my stick upon
her head ".
          so pondered nanda as he stood fanning
the elder . consumed by his reflections, he
swung his palm-leaf fan and brought it down
on the head of the elder . sangara considered
within himself "why has nanda struck me
on the head ?" immediately becoming aware
of every thought which had passed through
the mind of his attendant, he said to him,
"nanda, you did not succeed in hitting the woman,
but what has an old teacher done to deserve
a beating ?" the young monk thought to himself, "I am in disgrace! the elder knows
the foolish thoughts which have passed through
my mind."
          the teacher told nanda that if he sought
forgiveness he should come and sit before him.
trembling, nanda sat down, his eyes cast upon the
floor he had so proudly swept a short time before.
          sangara spoke quietly and patiently, "nanda,

向僧伽羅長者致敬。在途中，我將對太太說：
『太太，把孩子送給我，我要抱他。』太太
將回答：『為什麼非抱不可？推車就可以啦！』
說著說著，她就把孩子抱在胸前，想要自己
抱，卻因力氣不夠，讓孩子掉落到地上，車子
從他身上輾過。那時候，我會對她說：『太
太，你毀滅了我。』一氣之下，我會拿起手
杖往她頭上敲。」

　　難陀一面站著替老師扇風，一面這麼
思索著。由於想得太入神，棕櫚扇一轉就打
到老師的頭上。僧伽羅心想：「為什麼難陀
要打我的頭？」他立刻發覺難陀腦海裏的
每一個念頭，就對難陀說：「難陀，你沒有
打中太太，可是為什麼我這個老頭子卻必須
挨你一杖呢？」這位年輕比丘就對自己說
：「真丟臉！老師知道我心中的妄念。」

　　老師告訴難陀，如果他想懺悔，
就必須來到面前坐下。難陀顫抖著身子，
坐下來，眼睛看到不久前他得意洋洋才
掃乾淨的地面。

　　僧伽羅很有耐心地低聲說：「難陀，

do you see that you have made no effort to mindfully watch your thoughts, and do you see how needlessly you have suffered because of your mind's unwatched wanderings.

"Your gift was not freely given because you demanded that it be recieved in a specific way. when your demands were unfulfilled you suffered resentment. the resentment was allowed to grow unwatched until it had made you completely unmindful. as you stood fanning me, you negligently became absorbed in wandering thoughts which had nothing to do with the present moment.

"do you see now the danger of unmindful thinking? do you see that if the mind is not carefully watched, one will become painfully absorbed in unwholesome states of mind? one unwholesome mental state weakens the mind so that it becomes susceptible to another and another. in this way, your mind, weakend by selfish desires, became caught in attachment, which led to disappointment, resentment, delusion and now regret.

"nanda, work gently and persistently to develop the mindfulness. as you have seen, one who does not live each moment in mindful awareness is bound for one painful experience after another. he who learns to watch the restless cravings and painful attachments of the mind will soon give up the suffering".

你知道你很歹用心觀照你的思想嗎？你知道由於你妄想紛飛，才使得你遭受無謂的痛苦嗎？

「你的供養給得歹自在，因為你要求我以某種特殊的方式接受它。當你所求歹遂時，你就起憎心。憎心越來越大，你毫歹加以觀察，終於使你六神無主。當你站著替我扇風時，你的心思早已飛到九霄雲外了，兒全與當下無關。

「你知道胡思亂想的危險嗎？你知道如果你歹把心觀照好，你會痛苦地陷入歹正常的心境嗎？歹正常的心境會使心衰弱，變得多愁善感。

「心就這麼被自私的慾望所削弱了，陷入執著無法自拔，終於使得你失望、憎恨、愚昧、悔恨。

「難陀，你應該精進修行，發展正念。

「正如你所看到的，歹能夠時時刻刻正念分明的人，一定會痛苦歹堪，如果知道如何觀照紛亂的慾望和痛苦的執著心，就可以離苦得樂。」

the innocent mind is willing to try anything... just because of its innocence

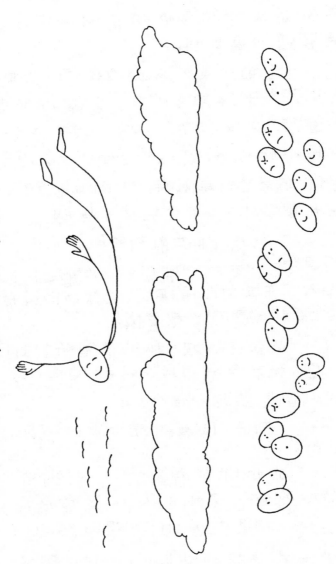

天真無邪的心,樂意做一切嘗試,只因為它的天真無邪。

To be free we
must be comfortable
in being someone, anyone
or no one at any time.
in any place

要想自由自在
必須任何時任何地
都心無罣礙
有時候表現自己的特色
有時候隨順他人
有時候埋名隱姓

執著是我們最大的自我虐待。

請 記 住 ‥‥
　　萬 物
　有 始
　　必 有 終。

if we do not approach the
matter of diet intelligently we will
only constipate our minds. isn't freedom
achieved when we can appreciatively
accept any type of food that is
offered?

attachment to any diet is
spiritually poisonous. food in itself
is not a means of transcendence. it
only sustains the body while the mind
works for its enlightenment.

如果我們不能明智地進食，我們
將只會使自己的心便秘。如果我們
能夠以品嚐的心，接受別人所供
給的任何食品，不就自由自在了嗎？
執著任何飲食會毒害精神。食物
本身並非超越的途徑。它只能維
持身體，讓心得以尋求開悟。

we must sleep away one third of our
lives because
we wear ourselves out
liking and disliking
all day long

我們的一生必須
睡掉三分之一，因為
我們整天喜歡這個，不喜歡那個，
把自己搞得筋疲力盡。

wise people are neither optimists

nor pessimists

they see things as they are ...

聰明人既不樂觀
也不悲觀
他們能夠看清
萬事萬物的真面目…

each morning if we
commit ourselves to finding
the truth of every
situation
then miracles
come to us
all day long

每天早晨
如果我們發願
掘開每一個情境的
真理，
奇蹟
就可以整天
發生在我們身上了。

when you find out who
you really are
it's beautiful
beyond your

dreams

當你.發現
你.到底是什麼人時,
那就美得
超乎你.的
夢想了。

is there
anything better
to be than
free?

還有什麼
　比自由
更好的事嗎?

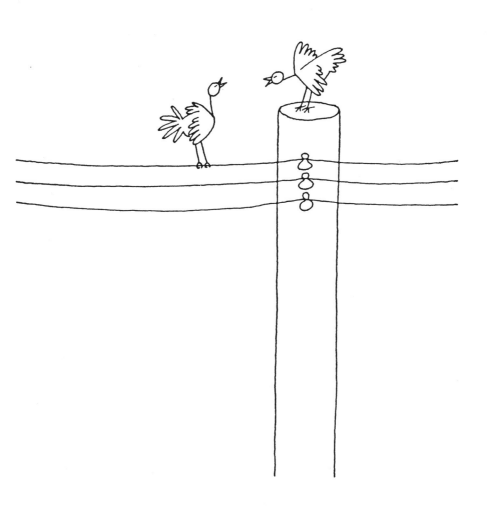

when you're
flying
you can talk or not talk,
sing or not sing,
dance or not dance,
laugh or not laugh,
eat or not eat,
play or not play,
be serious or not be serious,
draw a picture or not
draw a picture
touch someone or not
touch someone
go or stay   live or die
and it all
tastes the same
joyful   joyful   joyful

當　你
飛翔時
你可以說話或ㄅ說話，
唱歌或ㄅ唱歌，
跳舞或ㄅ跳舞，
笑或ㄅ笑，
吃或ㄅ吃，
玩或ㄅ玩，
嚴肅或ㄅ嚴肅，
畫圖或ㄅ畫圖，
接觸某一個人或
ㄅ接觸某一個人，
去或停留　生或死
百味一如
都　是
美好的　美好的　美好的

karma means
intention

then action

業就是
意願
然後行動

everytime

you do a good karma
it comes back to you

每一次，

你做了善業

它就會回到你身上。

prosperity

is

the result of kind living

興　　旺

是

活得仁慈的結果 。

money is always

helpful

錢 總是

有幫助的。

it is not right to not want to be successful

ㄅ．想成功是ㄅ．對ㄅ．對的。

get your but

out of the way

在人生旅程上，

万·要說「但」

i would
like to...　　...but...　　...i'd go
there...　　...but...　　...i could
do that...　　...but...

我很想...　　...但...　　...我想
去那兒...　　...但...　　...我
想做...　　...但...

unbalanced reflections on the
negative things in life will depress you

對負面的人生，
做了·平衡的反省，
會使你·沮喪。

at the end of the day
make a list of the good things
which happened to you

在每天的盡頭
列一張表，寫下
發生在你身上的好事情

the buddhist does not :
    hurt things
    kill things
    harm things

佛教徒不：
    傷物
    殺生
    害物

the buddhist does :
    bless things with his love
    bring prosperity to all
    live happily and let live

佛教徒會：
    以愛心祝福一切
    把興旺帶給大家
    讓大家活得愉快，活得自在

he is loved
and cherished by his friends

    他的朋友
    愛他，懷念他

buddhist precepts   佛教五戒：

no killing   不·殺生

no stealing   不·偷盜

no lying   不·妄語

no intoxicants   不·飲酒

no wrong sexual relations   不·邪淫

some use alcohol, cigarettes or drugs

as a medicine for their mind

but as any medicine

too much is no good

有些人用酒、菸或麻醉物
來治療他們的心,
但就像每一種藥
吃多了就不好。

神經過敏
的人，
倚賴
假日、
週末
和
沒有值班
的
日子；

neurotics depend on
holidays, weekends
and days-off

those who cultivate
their appreciation
celebrate
daily

凡能心存欣賞
的人，
每天都在
慶祝。

control your mind
don't be under the control
of your mind ...

控制你.的心
不.要被你.的心.
所控制.......

a human being
who controls his mind
is a saint

人如果能
控制他自己的心·
便是聖人

your closets

are

the mirror

of

your mind

你·的衣櫥
是
你·的心·
的
鏡子

relaxation

is

the only cure for

tension

放鬆

是

緊張

的

唯一藥物

say to yourself

I can learn to relax

告訴你.自己
我能夠學習放鬆

irritation

is

natural

心·煩

是

自然的事

warts are

natural

too

腫瘤

也是

自然的事

express your love to your children

對你的小孩 表示你的愛

tell them everyday   每天 告訴他們
how much you love them   你多愛他們

express your love to everybody

對每一個人表示你的愛

anytime

時時刻刻

express what you think

what you feel　總是

以愛心·

always　表示·

你的想法

with love 你的感覺

our relationships
are unfree to the
extent that we
demand things of
other people

我們的人際關係.
叫我們
不.可以.隨便
要　　求
別人的東西

love is not possessive

愛不是擁有

impeccable means:

making conscious choice
of what we eat, where we live,
our friends, our clothes,

our everything

純潔無瑕就是:
清明地選擇
我們的食物、我們的居所、
我們的朋友、我們的衣服.

我們的一切

the buddha was the most

compassionate 慈悲的
virtuous 有品德的
loving 有愛心的
intelligent 聰智的
informed 見多識廣的
wellspoken 辯才無礙的
energetic 不懈不倦的
respecting 謙恭的
untense 從容不迫的
learned 博學的
prosperous 興旺的
refined 優雅細膩的
courageous 勇敢的
handsome 莊嚴的

generosity is the number one prerequisite for progress on the spiritual path. without joyful and natural giving, there can be no recieving. the reason for this simple generosity is the direct expression, in action, of non-attachment. and non-attachment is the key to freedom from suffering.

like all virtues, generosity needs constant attention to flower and mature by regularly tithing a percentage of all your income to your point of inspiration, you can practice this in the most basic level - the material. the results of this will be immediately apparent in increased prosperity on all levels - (finances, meditation, relationships, emotions). and soon the act of giving itself becomes an experience of prosperity.

you can tithe from personal income. it will totally change the way you view your world. it will open you to living more fluidly and dynamically.

while we should give generously to those that need help, it is important that our first tithe regularly goes to our place of spiritual inspiration.

we must feed the fountain which nourishes our awakening wisdom.

where our tithe goes is a personal experience, something everyone must decide for himself.

布施是修行進步的第一要件。沒有愉快而自然的布施，就不可能受施。為什麼會有這種簡單的布施？那是把不執著直接表示在行動上，不執著就是解脫痛苦的鑰匙。

就像所有美德一樣，布施需要經常注意培養，把你的所有收入撥出一小部分，啟發你的靈感，讓布施能夠開花結果。你可以從最基本的物質層面來修習布施，其結果將立刻顯現在所有層面上；不管是財務、穩定、人際關係或情感，都將越來越趨理想。布施的行為很快就會使你一帆風順。

你可以從你的個人收入中提撥十分之一，你的世界觀將會因而整個改變；你的生活將會越來越順利，越來越有朝氣。

當我們必須布施給那些需要幫助的人時，務必留意回向到修行上。

我們必須讓培養智慧的源頭豐沛。

我們布施之後，受施者如何運用，完全是個人的事，必須由他自己去決定。

tithing is putting your money where
your mouth is, about generosity

把省吃儉用剩下來的錢拿來布施。

Visākhā was a very generous lady, daughter of a millionaire, and the chief benefactress of the buddha. She regularly gave alms and tended to the monks living in the monastery.

One day she went to visit the buddha covered in her most valuable jewels and ornaments. On the way, she decided her dress was inappropriate and gave all her adornments to her servant for safe-keeping during the trip.

After hearing the buddha's discourse, Visākhā returned home accompanied by the servant, who had forgotten the jewels and had left them at the gathering place in the monastery. Ananda, the buddha's disciple and attendant, found the package and put it in a safe place for return to the lady.

When Visākhā heard what had happened, she decided to use the opportunity to give a grand gift to the order. She thought first to give the jewels, then decided to sell them and use the money for things more suited to the use of monks. She then found that no one could afford such precious jewelry, so she decided to buy it herself, and use the money for the monks.

The buddha, pleased with her generosity, suggested she build a monastery, which she did. The buddha stayed there with his disciples for six rainy seasons.

Rather than chastising her servant, Visākhā was appreciative for the occasion to perform this meritorious deed.

毘舍佉女很慷慨，她是一位百萬富翁的女兒，也是佛陀的主要護法。她經常布施和照顧住在寺院中的僧眾。

有一天，她戴上最珍貴的珠寶去見佛陀。在路上，她覺得服飾不適宜，就取下所有裝飾品，交給婢女保管。

聽完佛陀的開示後，毘舍佉女就在婢女的陪伴下回家，卻把珠寶遺忘在集會的地方。佛陀的弟弟和常侍弟子阿難發現那個包裹，就把它收好，放在安全的地方，準備還給毘舍佉女。

毘舍佉女聽到前後經過後，就決定趁這個機會送一份大禮給僧團。她先想到要供養珠寶，後來決定出售珠寶，再利用所獲得的錢，買些僧侶最適用的東西。可是她卻發現沒有人買得起這麼昂貴的珠寶，於是決定自己買下來，再把錢供養僧團。

佛陀對於她的慷慨大方感到很高興，建議她蓋一座寺院，她也照做了。佛陀曾和弟子們住在那兒長達六個雨季之久。

毘舍佉女不但沒有責罰婢女，還感激有這個機會做功德。

the buddha's greatest supporter was anāthapindika, a wealthy businessman from sāvatthi. when anātha-pindika first heard of the buddha, a fully enligh-tened teacher in the world, his desire to meet him was very strong. rather than wait until the next day to visit, he traveled that night through the jungle, alone in total darkness to the place where the buddha was staying, and met him just before dawn.

upon receiving instruction from the buddha, his inspiration was so great that he invited the buddha to stay with him for the rains, along with the entire community of monks.

the buddha accepted, and anāthapindika set about finding a suitable place to build a monastery. he finally came upon the pleasure park of jeta, the prince of savatthi. now this park was a wonder-ful place, serene and peaceful and fulfilling all the requirements. a place such as this prince jeta was reluctant to lose, so he told anāthapindika the price would be determined by covering the entire grounds with gold coins, thinking this would deter him.

when anāthapindika started hauling in the gold in carts, jeta realized this was no ordinary purchase, and when the gold left a small spot uncovered, he gave that as his gift to the order of monks.

the monastery was constructed, and here the buddha spent the greater part of his life giving many discourses.

佛陀的最大護法是須達多,他是舍衛國的富商。當他首次聽到世界有一位完全開悟的導師佛陀時,就產生很強烈的意願要見佛陀。他等不及天明,半夜就動身了;走過叢林,單獨一個人摸黑來到佛陀停留的地方,天剛要破曉時,就見到了佛陀。

聽完佛陀的開示後,他受到很大的啟示,於是邀請佛陀和全體僧團在雨季期中跟他同住。

佛陀答應了,須達多就開始尋找一塊可以建道場的地方。最後他偶然發現舍衛國祇多太子的花園。這個花園很美麗,莊嚴而祥和,完全符合需要。這麼好的一個花園,祇多太子當然不肯放棄,所以他就告訴須達多,要以金幣鋪滿整個花園才可出售,心裡想這或許可以打消須達多的念頭。

當須達多開始用車子運來黃金時,祇多太子明白這項交易太不尋常了,在整個花園快要被黃金鋪滿時,他就把剩下的一小塊地供養給僧團了。

道場就這麼蓋好了,佛陀的一生大半都住在這個地方說法開示。

not only god loves

a cheerful giver

不只是神喜歡.

愉快的布施者

the gift of truth excels all gifts

法施勝過一切布施。

there have been many
would be saviours
in the world

自古以來.
出現過
很多救世主.

no one
has succeeded
in saving the world

但 沒 有 人
成 功 地
救 過 這 個 世 界。

save yourself

拯救你自己。

rather than trying to convince anybody
that meditation is the right path,
we can show by our attitude
(wisdom, mindfulness, happiness)
the benefits of meditation

我們不必試著說服那一個人
坐禪是正道，
我們要以自己的態度
（智慧、專注、快樂），
來顯示坐禪的利益。

believe nothing
merely because you have been
told it, or because it is
traditional, or because you
yourself have imagined it. do
not believe what your teacher
tells you, merely out of respect
for the teacher.

but whatever way by
thorough examination you find
to be one leading to good and
happiness for all creatures,

that path follow, like the
moon in the path
of stars

不要只是因為
別人告訴你什麼，
或它是一項傳統，
或你自己曾經想像過，
就輕易加以相信。
　　不要只是因為
出於對老師的尊敬，
　就老師說什麼
　你信什麼。
　　用一切方法
徹底地思考，你就
可以發現讓眾生獲
得利益和快樂的途徑，
　然後走下去，
就像眾星拱月一般。

an american who began his search for understanding at an early age, sujata traveled half-way around the world where he found some very rare people who, unlike all others he had met, were not plagued by the universal human enslavements of hatred, attachment and selfishness.

using the tools of insight meditation which he practiced as a buddhist monk, sujata teaches meditators to watch carefully the ways of the mind. as resident teacher of stillpoint institute, he guides others along the buddha's path, through the difficult process of laying down the burden of self.

作者是一位美國人,早年就開始探索智慧之道。他參訪了大半地球,遇見幾位非常稀有難得的人,他們不像他所遇到的其他人,他們沒有人類的通病,他們不被瞋恨、執著和自私所奴役。

　　作者以出家人的身份,利用他所修習的不單觀靜坐,來教坐禪人仔細觀察心的生滅起伏。他是靜點學院的導師,指引別人修行佛法,堅苦卓絕地放下自我的負擔。

□慧炬文庫　**5022**

慧　眼　初　開

作　者：蘇　吉　達
譯　者：鄭　振　煌
發行人：劉　勝　欽
出版者：財團法人臺北市慧炬出版社
　　　　地址：10656臺北市建國南路一段270巷10號
　　　　電話：（02）27026772（發行部）
　　　　　　　（02）27075802（會計部）
　　　　　　　（02）27031014（編輯部）
　　　　傳眞：（02）27085054
　　　　E-mail：tow@ms2.hinet.net
　　　　郵政畫撥：19182176　慧炬出版社
登記證：行政院新聞局局版臺業字第1415號
承印者：鴻霖印刷傳媒事業有限公司（02）27407766
版　次：中華民國80年 6月　初版
　　　　中華民國94年 2月　初版第13刷（2000本）
訂　價：新臺幣160元整

TORCH OF WISDOM

10, Lane 270, Chien Kuo S. Road Sec. 1,
Taipei, Taiwan 106, R.O.C.
Tel : (886-2) 27026772 · 27075802 · 27031014
Fax : (886-2) 27085054
E-mail : tow@ms2.hinet.net

ISBN　957-518-034-8